The Fire Eater and the Bearded Lady

poems by

Sally Albiso

Finishing Line Press
Georgetown, Kentucky

The Fire Eater and the Bearded Lady

ACKNOWLEDGMENTS

I would like to thank Suzann Bick, Mary-Alice Boulter, Carmen Germain, Molly
Hollenbach, Patrick Loafman, and Diana Somerville for their close reading of
these poems and encouragement.

Publisher: Leah Maines

Editor: Christen Kincaid

Cover Art: John Robert Albiso

Author Photo: John Robert Albiso

Cover Design: John Robert Albiso

Printed in the USA on acid-free paper.
Order online: www.finishinglinepress.com
          also available on amazon.com

Author inquiries and mail orders:
Finishing Line Press
P. O. Box 1626
Georgetown, Kentucky 40324
U. S. A.

Table of Contents

For Suzann, who so readily ran away to the circus with me

Ladies and Gentlemen, Boys and Girls, Children of All Ages

I will orchestrate your days
and nights, fill them
with parading elephants
and pacing lions
whose roar contains a darkness
that will wake you,
weeks from now,
to pant at shadows
and be thankful
you're only a witness
to courage. Come.
Jugglers and clowns wait,
nimble hands and faces.
Acrobats and sideshow oddities.
Even a mind-reader
who bares your thoughts.
The circus exposes us all.
I in top hat and frock coat,
you in Sunday best
entering my house of worship
and believing
the apocalypse has arrived:
wild beasts leap
through rings of fire;
horsemen race
on white, red, black,
and ashen mounts;
aerialists take wing
like annunciating angels. Come.
For a trifling price,
I will be your prophet,
reveal wondrous and fearful sights
as trumpets blare.

The Fire Eater and the Bearded Lady

You insist it doesn't hurt to swallow flame.
Exhale it like a dragon or demon.
Ignite a torch without a match

approaching what consumes without fear
and holding it in your mouth. You kiss me
like a wick, my lips your wax

yet are careful not to singe my whiskered cheeks.
For you suffer the opposite fate,
hairless as a Chinese Crested Dog,

exposed skin flushing as if seared.
Nothing grows there, not even the finest down.
An auspicious turn given your profession.

Still your lash-less gaze delights
in my abundance other men scorn
and you groom me like a pet

from eyebrows to feet, murmur *hirsute*
as an endearment. You drape my beard
across your head when cold,

worry it through your fingers when thinking
and weave gifts into its length:
a pair of ruby hoops to blush in my ears,

the petals of yellow roses
to affirm your jealousy. I bought you a wig
dark as the soot left on my pillow,

made from real hair like a mourner's memento.
But it caught on fire as if part of the act.
You used your flaring scalp to light a cigar,

transferred the flame with an index finger
before putting it out with your tongue
coarse as a cat's.

My sweet, I've felt the blisters,
tasted the scorched pulp there,
know you burn like the rest of us.

Girl-to-Gorilla (And Back)

The most popular show—
a young woman transforms into an ape—

an illusion we choose to believe.
See how her brow ridge protrudes,

nose flattens, hair darkens and grows
until no flesh is visible

but the furrowed skin of face, palms,
soles. She walks on all fours

approaching the middle of the stage,
silently regards us.

Has she lost the ability to speak,
her understanding of the past?

The spot-lighted present all that matters?
Someone throws her a banana.

Someone beats his chest.
Clichés she ignores, opposable thumbs

pushing against the floor's thin veneer.
No costume this.

Nothing between us but our image
we seek in her gaze. The amber distance

before we gained our bipedal stance,
the fur retreated,

length of limbs unfurled.
And we stood upright as she does

once more, pale skin revealed
in spangled majorette dress.

We gasp. She yawns as if this occurs
daily—her evolution, our own.

Cage Hand

It was the giraffe
pummeling his way into light
kicking a hole in the pen
the size of possibility,
of distances eyed from his height
and air tongued through wooden slats.

The camel following,
the zebras, and miniature ponies.
Their hooves testing sawdust and dirt
until pavement grew firm beneath them
and they wandered
among drowsy neighborhoods:

the vision of parading animals
summoned as if by another flood.
The people still throaty with night,
the children who'd insisted all along
the circus could suddenly appear
when they were asleep,

forced into the rigidity of bedtime
where dreams couldn't compare
to morning's reverie
turning a corner onto their street.
I was among those sent
to round up the escaped:

the zebras flashing
like black-and-white newsreels,
the two-humped Bactrian camel
swaying down avenues
empty as deserts,
trotting ponies no larger than dogs.

But the giraffe still roamed,
accounts of his head floating
above roofs, the antennae of his horns.
Then he faded away. I imagined him
bent over a backyard pool,
front legs splayed so he could drink,

or lured with apples into some hidden place.
We questioned the kids.
One in particular
whose pockets were stuffed with hay,
a gamey odor rising.
We combed garages and barns,

private grounds and public gardens,
fields on the edge of town.
How could a giraffe disappear,
sixteen feet tall
and covered in reticulated spots?
His vanishing more improbable

than the magician's act
as the morning waned
and he hadn't been found.
Nor that afternoon when dusk fell
and the wet dark drew him in.
His long silhouette ghosting the reach

of cedars where he could take cover,
mimic their stillness while we searched,
called his name, left a trail of carrots
as bait. Though what would
tempt him more, food
or that fenceless night, I couldn't say.

The Circus Elephant Remembers

her family's frantic calls
rumbling through her bones.

The horizon drawing close as a net.
Scent of humans like dung or baboon.
A dart's quick wound.

How she fell into a dreamless sleep
and woke to what could only be dream—

a high-pitched voice issuing commands:
Come here. Lie down. Up.
Hold this. Let that go.

But she embraces the memory
of other sounds. The rasp of grasslands

tormented by wind, their greening
after the monsoons. How the moon ripened
and night proffered its seed,

the matriarch led them toward water.
A man directs her days now

as if her mother, sister, aunt.
Yet they share no blood
and the lessons he teaches profit only him.

She could refuse his orders,
the bull hook and chains,

ram his body instead. Trample it
until he no longer moves.
But that would leave the others mourning

the dirt holding her scent
as she once lingered over the skeletons

of her dead, brittle as the sky during drought
and white-hot to the touch
as if all sorrow smoldered there.

Spidora

He knows it's a trick—
the lady's head emerging
from a spider's body
larger than his own—
but he wants it to be true.

For her web to stretch
over the tent
dappling doorways, its weave,
and her eight limbs
to truss the audience

in silk. Any movement
focusing her attention,
that painted mouth, fangs
hidden beneath a smile.
He notes the bloody shape

on her abdomen
as she blows toxic kisses
from multiple palms
shooting white filaments
into the front row. One lands

on him, sticky as pitch,
and he grows still as if bound.
A deafening buzz in his ears
like flies the size of cats
are suspended next to him,

their compound eyes
faceting his own death.
He shivers, recalls the effects
of venom. A black widow
hidden in his sheets as he slept,

her bite rising like a dream
to consciousness.
A blistering wound
on his palm, a scarred crater
with concentric lines

a fortune-teller could read,
predict pain
shattering innocence
like Eden's snake.
How he flared with fever, floated

where dark distances converge,
released from the soiled
garden of his body.
A sensation he wants to feel again—
that freedom betrayal bestows.

Sword Swallower

The act my wife begs to see
then cannot watch

closing her eyes and grabbing her throat
as if the blade chokes her.

How is it done? she asks
gagging. I don't know the answer.

How anything sharp is swallowed,
fatal wounds concealed.

The sword swallower devours a dagger
until only the hilt remains.

My wife peeks from behind her hands
as he attempts a scimitar, its curve

much more difficult to take in. She pales
but gazes fully now,

arches her neck
and opens her mouth wide

as if to gorge on that warped weapon too,
consume what cuts and not bleed.

The Lion Tamer

Cats not tamed but trained.
Isn't that what we do to the wild among us?
A chair, a whip can't stop what's been unleashed—
even a gun fired too late.
There must be a willingness to back down.
Roar and lash at air but not attack.
Lower your eyes first.
Jump through rings of fire when commanded.
Still some not so easily tutored,
the scars on my body a hard-won lesson—
always face a predator.
The rank panting of death I draw near,
my eyes wide, pulse rapid, muscles tense.
How closely fear imitates love.

Roustabout

He puts things up
and takes them down, rouses
canvas and poles, hay and manure.

He follows from place to place.
But secretly he longs to fly
like the trapeze artists

climbing the rigging—
grandparents to grandchildren.
Even the youngest fearless

of heights. She launches
from her father's shoulders
into her mother's embrace,

refuses gravity's pull
tumbling through air.
The nets some consolation

though a back can still be shattered,
a neck. He cranes
to watch the aerialists take flight

as if the reach of their bodies
can't contain them.
He only scales ladders,

strings wires like skeins of muscle,
erects platforms to stand
where they leap—

his breath quickening,
stomach lurching
as if he hangs from a trapeze

upside down and must break
another's fall
with perfect timing. He tries

to hold on. Keeps the skeleton
of a mouse in his pocket,
its flesh stripped by ants, and imagines

becoming that small yet strong
enough to bear a greater weight
into the swarming silence.

Lazarus

I sniff at wind like any dog,
fetch, lick hands
washing them clean, beg
only for what's easily given.

Yet I'm a wonder
as my name implies:
leaping onto a galloping pony
and off again,

jumping through hoops,
performing a handstand,
barking the correct answer
to mathematical problems

as my trainer alerts me.
(A subtle blink
no one else sees.)
I also sing and dance.

But my best trick is playing dead:
staggering around the arena
as if kicked by hooves
then falling onto my back,

all four legs in the air, tongue lolling
while the audience grows still
as my tail. The spotlight lingers
on my limp body.

The trainer kneels and urges
everyone to pray for a miracle.
Such a bowing of heads.
Even the other dogs in the act

sitting up, one by one,
positioning their front paws
in supplication until,
on command, I'm resurrected.

The Magician's Daughter

What if I really did levitate,
flat on my back,

arms crossed over my chest
like the dead? Floated
off the stage and down the aisle

as ladies fainted,
gentlemen narrowed their eyes?

Drifted out of the building
and up like another moon
defying night?

Or if I were truly sawn in half:
legs and feet sundered,

mind and heart still tethered
to the illusion of my mother
who died giving birth.

A debt I cannot repay
though I make myself small

to be tucked into a trunk
and disappear. Never flinch
as Father throws knives at me.

Bucket Boy

Someone has to muck out stalls,
keep the Big Top clean,

follow the ass-end
of animals—

manure less objectionable
than human stink.

The scent of hay and grain,
fields where the sun burns

constant and cotton is picked
until palms cramp

around the pale flowering
of that harvest.

I've chosen another servitude.
Still bend beneath sky

but am not cowed.
Today I enter a tiger's cage

when by mistake
the animal is returned too soon,

a hose my only weapon.
I remain silent

trying to tame my feral heart.
The tiger focuses its gaze

patient as men
who wait for prey—

their hands curling into claws,
their smiles into teeth.

But this is no lynching. No corpse
hanging where crows gather.

An impersonal death,
they'd find only parts of me.

The tiger chuffs as if calling a cub
to a kill. Light silhouettes

the iron bars containing us.
I point the hose like a gun,

its stream issuing,
reach for the closed gate

at my back. Slowly, slowly
the way predators stalk.

Human Torso

His act: to have survived.
Costumed in christening gown and bonnet
like a baby, he's spoon-fed,

given a bottle of milk laced with brandy
so he sits calmly and smiles,
impresses the audience

with the eloquence of his speech:
Shakespeare's sonnets,
Lincoln's Gettysburg Address

recited in his sonorous voice.
For he's no infant but a grown man
lacking arms or legs.

How light his body without their weight.
How heavy, unable to be moved
unless assisted, held close

like something unwieldy or precious.
When he thinks of two it's eyes and ears,
nostrils. How he sees, hears, breathes

like any other, dreams. His sleep filled
with creatures devoid of hands and feet:
worms and snakes drifting

along the ground or through water.
No need for opposable thumbs,
prehensile toes

but the amniotic warmth of baths
in which he floats freely,
suspended there as if unborn.

Sideshow

We submitted to the machine on exhibit,
marveled at our exposed bones.
Radiation just a word.
Less harmful than the sun's gaze.

We stood in long lines to glow
like the displayed
fish, frogs, and rabbits,
their beating hearts bared—

the solidity of flesh an illusion—
peered at the x-rayed skeleton
of a girl. Her bones ossified
like Lot's wife.

Her skull twisted to one side
as if she forever looks
over her shoulder
at the place she's been forced

to abandon, watches it burn,
hands crystallizing, heart brining.
Her rigid stillness opposing those
who only look forward,

who refuse to face
the lost. We didn't understand
this invention, white light
that can poison blood

like forbidden knowledge,
and sought its revelation
many times—our undoing.
Both of us taking to bed,

clumps of hair littering the pillow,
sores in our mouths, a weakness.
You bleeding from your nose,
I from somewhere far deeper.

We should have known the danger
in such hubris. To think we could see
beneath the surface of skin like gods
and not be punished.

Clown

I'm either greeted with joy
or fear, children crying
at my extravagant smile, eyebrows
winging like flushed birds.
Even a pie to my face
doesn't please them.
But I'm meant to act the fool,
make you happy. Sometimes
I play characters:
a bumbling cop who ends up
locked behind bars;
a butcher chasing others
with a rubber cleaver
that cuts nothing;
a sad-sack whose sorrow I paint on,
begin to blubber
wiping my nose on a spectator's tie.
A favorite gag. How I pretend
to trust others while the butt
of their jokes. How I'll do anything
for a laugh.

Conjoined

Siamese twins we call them.
Freaks. Deities.

Fish-man, two-headed woman.
Shiva with his many arms.

A sideshow, carnival act,
torsos wedded in perpetual embrace,

faces melded like masks
of tragedy and comedy.

Thought or death their only isolation.
To remove one is to sacrifice

the other. Such separation our need
not theirs. The burden of assigning souls

to those feared as monstrous,
pitied for their visceral union

while we take the measure
of our unshared hearts.

High Wire

Always this division—
those rooted to earth
as they gaze skyward

but never leave firm ground,
even buried
beneath a mantle of dirt,

and those who pose like light
on day's ledge, place one foot
before the other, don't look down.

The acrobat leans over her feet,
uses only her arms
as counterweight, sways.

But she's no tree
to endure the assault of wind
and remain upright.

No bird with bones buoyant enough
to gain lift. She feels her way
across, wades

through the liquidity of air
as if treading a path
between walls of water

and their release—
and all of pharaoh's army behind her,
bellow of the tide returning

while ahead the struggle
toward belief. She wavers
as if bowing before the unseen.

The audience holds its breath.
So trying, this act of faith,
this bearing witness.

Sally Albiso earned a BA in Spanish from UCLA and an MA in English with a creative writing emphasis from San Diego State University. While at SDSU, she studied with the poets Glover Davis and Carolyn Forché and completed a thesis of her own poetry.

After receiving her master's degree, she taught English composition, creative writing, and English as a Second Language at Chapman College, San Diego State University Extension, and Southwestern College.

In 2003, Albiso and her husband moved from California to the North Olympic Peninsula of Washington State, where she returned to writing poetry. She has been nominated for two Pushcart Prizes and received the Jeanne Lohmann Poetry Prize, The Muriel Craft Bailey Memorial Award, the Robert Frost Foundation Poetry Award, and the Camber Press Chapbook Award for her chapbook *Newsworthy*. Another chapbook, *The Notion of Wings*, was published by Finishing Line Press in 2015. Her poems have appeared in *Blood Orange Review, Crab Creek Review, Floating Bridge Review, Poetica, Pontoon: an anthology of Washington State poets, Rattle, The Comstock Review* and other publications.